Crystal Healing for Beginners

The Complete Guide to Unleashing the Power of Crystal Healing

Lara Barlett

Table of Contents

Introduction

Crystal healing is a popular art that has its roots in ancient civilisations such as Ancient Egypt, Ancient Greece, India and the Roman Empire. The very first references to the use of crystals in healing rituals occurred during the Ancient Sumerian civilisation.

Many of these civilisations mined precious stones and crystals, using them in jewellery – including amulets and healing talismans – as protective charms or during rituals to maximise the potential of their metaphysical properties.

Several crystal names have their origins in languages such as Greek. For example, "amethyst" originates from the Ancient Greek word meaning "not drunk." This was because it was often used as a charm to prevent drunkenness or heal the effects of a hangover. Similarly, "hematite" is named after the Greek word for blood due to its red hue. It was often worn by Greek sailors to protect them when they were at sea.

By the late 17th century, crystals and stones had been used for a multitude of purposes. At this time, as the Enlightenment swept across Europe, enthusiasts started to dismiss the superstitions that had previously been associated with crystals. Before the Age of Enlightenment, crystals often carried *magical* connotations. After this time, scientists started to conduct experiments to explore the tangible effects that crystals demonstrated when used for healing.

With the arrival of the 19th century came the advent of western crystal healing as we know it today. This art grew and developed during the next 200 years, reaching a peak in the 1980s, when New Age culture collided with ancient cultures. Utilising many of the old traditions, healers explored and developed an art that culminated in the perfection of crystal healing and the use of precious and semi-precious stones in therapeutic methods.

In the modern-day, crystal therapy is often used in a complementary way to western medicine, to heal the body and the mind. After centuries on the periphery of medicine, many physicians have now welcomed the use of crystals into the mainstream.

Crystals are formed in nature from different atoms, compounds and elements. For example, a diamond is considered a crystal – albeit an extremely expensive one. Natural diamonds are formed over time from carbon in the presence of extreme heat and pressure. Many other crystals and stones are also formed in a similar manner. You can find brittle, soft and harder stones, many of which possess healing properties.

Crystals are excellent for use on their own to ward off negative energy or to keep your energy in balance. They can also be used alongside other alternative techniques such as breathing exercises or yoga poses to help you channel the positive energy of your crystals through your body and cleanse yourself of detrimental negative energy.

Crystals are used for healing both physical and emotional ailments. They have been successfully utilised in fields such as pain control and the easing of mental health problems like depression and anxiety. It is essential to note that crystals can be used on their own or in combination with modern medicine. They are an excellent way to heal yourself, using your own inner energy.

When you choose your crystals, you may find yourself drawn to specific stones and it is important to trust your instinct. Your crystals will be in tune with *you* and your energy field. Essentially, they are on your wavelength.

In this book, you will learn about the kinds of crystals that are available and what they can be used for. You will also discover how to use them effectively, both in passive and active use to heal you physically and emotionally as well as learning to understand their array of wonderful qualities.

How Do Crystals Work For Healing The Mind And Body?

Crystals can work on healing your mind and body in a variety of ways. These include:

- Increasing your energy levels

- Protect you from negative energy

- Cleanse bad energy

- Unblocking and rebalancing your energy

- Lightening your aura

Your body and mind have several energy centres throughout. In eastern culture, these are known as the chakras. There are seven major chakras, although many proponents believe there are more than 1000 minor chakras.

When your energy becomes blocked in your energy centres or chakras, you can experience negative physical and emotional symptoms. Crystals can draw this negative energy out of your body, essentially acting as a magnet to remove it and cleanse your body.

However, it is important to remember that the mind is also a powerful tool in crystal healing. Alongside the power of the crystals, focusing on the healing field of the crystal is extremely important. Visualisation and mindfulness can be used to achieve this effectively. Both visualisation and mindfulness can be used with any stone to help to heal any physical or mental ailment.

Your brain has spent an entire lifetime being "hardwired" in a specific way. This is as a result of all your experiences – both good and bad. Crystals, in combination with visualisation and mindfulness, can assist you in rewiring the connections in the brain to overcome past and current traumas. Your brain's ability to change is known as *neuroplasticity.* The combination of your brain's powerful energy, as well as the healing energy field of crystals, is ideal for ensuring that you can recover and heal from mental troubles such as anxiety, depression, obsessive-compulsive disorder, eating disorders and self-destructive behaviours.

You can now try these first two practice activities, to help you get used to using crystals for healing. These simple introductory activities are easy to perform and very effective for helping you to tune your mind and harmonise yourself with your crystals. The visualisation practice is a good way to start learning how to heal physical problems while the mindfulness practice is perfect for starting to heal emotional disorders.

General visualisation practice

1. Find a quiet, calm place and take a seated position.

2. Hold your crystal in your hand, place it on your lap or on a nearby surface close to you.

3. Focus on the crystal and feel how it vibrates and hums with energy.

4. Imagine that energy is a bright, white light surrounding the crystal.

5. Visualise the bright light leaving the crystal and flowing into your body, specifically flowing into the part of your body that is afflicted by pain or trauma.

6. Hold the light inside you. Picture that light as a warm, restorative force renewing and rejuvenating you.

7. Allow the light to flow from you, taking any dark energy with it and returning the darkness to the crystal.

Mindfulness practice

1. Take your crystal into your hand and stare down at the crystal, taking in the colours of the crystal. Does it have any stripes or mottling? Does it shine or is it dull?

2. Rub your fingers across the surface of the stone. Notice the details on the stone and whether it is rough or smooth. Consider the shape of the stone and its size.

3. Repeat the process, looking and feeling the crystal as you will notice new details of its look and feel all the time.

4. Ensure that your focus remains on the crystal at all times. If you notice that your mind begins to wander, bring your attention back to the crystal.

Mindfulness is excellent for distracting you from negative thoughts and refocusing your mind. It is also a good way to stop worrying and lessen anxiety. When you feel that your anxiety levels are high, try this practice as it can calm your heart rate and breathing, as well as lessen racing thoughts. If you are prone to self-destructive or impulsive behaviours, keep your crystal with you at all times so that you can practice this technique rather than acting out in a negative way.

In addition to using the crystals actively, you can also use them as "passive" healers. That is to say, you can keep crystals around you, using them to draw negative energy out of the environment around you. Crystals can absorb negative energy from you.

- Keep crystals in a room where you spend a lot of time – such as your living room, kitchen or bedroom.
- Wear a crystal in a necklace, bracelet or ring.
- Place a crystal under your pillow when you sleep.
- Place protective crystals into your car or take them with you when you travel.

- Take a crystal to your workplace to temper your stress levels when you are at work.

These are all environments where you may experience negative energy build-up and environments that often need to be cleansed of bad energy. By keeping the crystals close to you, you may start to notice that your physical and emotional symptoms lessen, you find yourself with a lighter and more positive mood and you enjoy higher energy and motivation levels.

Of course, everyone's physical and emotional symptoms are different. Various crystals can help you to heal in different ways. Therefore, choosing the appropriate crystal for you is extremely important. In the next chapter, you will discover all the different varieties of crystals, allowing you to select the right crystal for your individual needs.

The Ultimate Guide To Crystals

Choosing your very first crystals can be a daunting task when you consider the vast variety of stones that are available. There are many different types and subtypes of crystals but each crystal has its own benefits and can be used in a different way. Some crystals have multiple uses and they are extremely versatile.

While there are hundreds of crystals, and this is just a small sample of them, this guide will help you to gain a grounding and understanding of some of the most common, popular and affordable crystals that you can find.

Obsidian: This popular crystal had a plethora of protective characteristics. It is often used to provide a shield to combat negativity in both the physical and emotional spheres. If you are emotionally blocked or your emotional energy is suffering from an imbalance, obsidian can help to cleanse you and stabilise your emotional energy.

Obsidian is associated with characteristics such as compassion, empathy, clarity of mind and mental strength and resilience. It is often used to heal problems of the digestive system, including cramping, pain and indigestion. These crystals tend to be jet-black but you may occasionally find mottled obsidian or brown and red varieties of the stone.

Jasper: A beautiful ruby red stone, that is occasionally also found in a yellow, green, brown or even a blue hue, Jasper is a stone from the quartz family. It is a crystal that is extremely empowering to its users and can help you to boost confidence in yourself.

Jasper is the perfect crystal for absorbing negative energy and creating a protective field around you to ward off negative vibes. It is associated with mental focus, raised levels of confidence and promoting bravery.

Rose Quartz: A stone that is excellent for channelling love and cleansing the body of negative emotions, Rose Quartz can restore more positive emotions and transform your mindset. It allows you to gain a sense of balance and harmony in your heart and promotes trust in intimate relationships.

What's more, it is ideal for use as a calming and comforting stone, especially when you are suffering from the wake of low mood or traumas. An added advantage of this stone is that it promotes self-belief and confidence.

Clear Quartz: When it comes to physical and emotional healing, Clear Quartz is considered to be one of the world's most masterful stones. Clear quartz is perfect for helping to regulate the levels of positive and negative energy in your body by cleansing negativity and transforming your energy to positive. It can be used to help achieve balance in the body and mind as well as boosting the immune system.

Clear Quartz is often used in combination with other stones as it is adept at amplifying the energy of related crystals. For example, clear quartz and rose quartz can be used together to enhance the power of rose quartz and strengthen its abilities.

Amethyst: Perfect for purifying the spirit, healing physical ailments and protecting yourself from negativity, amethyst is also associated with achieving emotional wisdom and promoting sobriety. In the times of Ancient Greece, it was used to heal the physical and mental aftereffects of a hangover. It has long been associated with sincerity and truth.

For sufferers of insomnia, amethyst is widely used as a tool to relieve stress surrounding a lack of nighttime slumber. As well as positive emotional benefits, it can aid pain relief, lessen anxiety and help to cleanse the blood of toxins. It is also excellent at helping to boost the levels of hormones in your body, ensuring that you maintain a healthy and balance physical state.

Citrine: Citrine is often associated with optimism and hope. This is epitomised by its bright yellow hue and shiny surface colour. It can enhance your mood, purge pessimism and enrich every aspect of your life with joy and wonder.

Citrine is often utilised to boost enthusiasm and motivation in the face of depression and anxiety or trauma. It is excellent at eradicating fear and transforming your mindset from a low, unhappy one to a much more mindful and inspirational one. What's more, it can be used to heal a fragmented focus and promote concentration.

Tiger's Eye: Tiger's Eye is considered to be a harmonising stone. It is often seen in a golden colour but may also be dark shades of reddish-brown. It is a silky lustre and often extremely mottled.

This stone is often used to boost motivation and imbue yourself with power, especially if you have been stuck in a cycle of self-doubt. It can be used to heal yourself following relationship traumas and promote healthy and ambitious career aspirations.

Turquoise: An extremely grounding stone, turquoise is a rich aqua-blue colour. It is often used in jewellery to bring good luck and attract positive vibrations. Additionally, it can rebalance your emotions, ensuring that you stay grounded and connected to yourself.

Turquoise is a good stone for physical healing too. If you have problems with your immune system, respiratory issues or bone and joint ailments, turquoise is an excellent choice to help improve these conditions and encourage your body to heal itself.

Sapphire: Sapphires tend to be a deep, rich royal blue in colour and often reflect the wisdom they can endow on their owners. They are associated with prosperity, joy and peace and can help people to attain prosperity. If your creative centres and intuition feel blocked, sapphires are a good choice for releasing the blockage and allowing your mind to open more freely to the beauty in the world around you.

Physically, these stones can benefit you on multiple levels. Sapphires have often been used to treat health problems regarding the blood, eyes and cells. They also have emotional benefits and are well used as healing crystals to combat anxiety, depression and insomnia.

Moonstone: Moonstones are focused on promoting inner growth by strengthening yourself and building up your resilience. This opalescent stone is found in a variety of shades and colours, including green, pink and peach as well as a colourless variety. These stones create an esoteric, protective field around you. It is famed for helping to generate a new beginning.

It is linked with balancing yourself, finding your intuition and learning to trust yourself. It is a feminine crystal and can be used particularly well by women who want to get in touch with their inner femininity, channelling it and taking the benefits of it. Like the moon itself, it is a tranquil body and moonstones can help you to harness this lunar power.

Bloodstone: This crystal comes in a variety of shades and styles. As its name indicates, it is often used to helping to remove toxins from the blood and is therefore often used to heal blood disorders and promote improved circulation.

Emotionally, it is used to stimulate excellent levels of creativity and inspiration. Often used as a tool to achieve mindfulness, bloodstone can help to heal aggression, lack of patience and sensations of irritability.

Ruby: Rubies are brimming with energy and they can help you to boost your own levels of positive energy. These deep red gemstones are often associated with sexuality and sensuality, helping to restore and improve low libido. Essentially, they can help you to rediscover lost vitality.

Another use of rubies is for motivating the mind and boosting your intellect. They can be used to clear your mind so you can focus on the truth and achieve a higher level of self-awareness and introspectiveness.

For physical healing, the main use of rubies is to make improvements to ailments of the circulatory system. It is an excellent stone for detoxifying the blood and treating conditions such as anaemia.

Celestite: One of the most multipurpose stones, celestite can be used to stimulate multiple systems in the body. Its serene blue colour is associated with both intuition and communication. It can help to boost your wisdom and comprehension of both your inner self and those around you.

Celestite is an excellent meditation stone and works perfectly when used in mindfulness practices. It is useful for helping your body to purge physical and spiritual toxins and heal disorders that are located in the upper body.

Black Onyx: An extremely calming and grounding stone, black onyx is often used to heal intense emotions of grief or substantial and chronic worrying. It is generally linked with establishing wisdom and attaining perspective. Black onyx can help you to find your centre when you are struggling and feel lost.

It is often used for treating problems with your bones, blood, teeth, feet and bone marrow. Green onyx, a different but similar form of the stone can be used for similar purposes. However, while black onyx is linked with the base chakra, green onyx is linked with the heart chakra.

Choosing Your Crystals

Once you are familiar with the various properties of crystals, it is essential to take some steps so that you select the right crystal for you. Generally, you might just want to passively use crystals. If this is the case, opt for protective crystals such as obsidian or jasper.

However, if you have a specific problem that you want to treat, follow these steps to choose your crystal.

1. Identify the problem

Knowing what is wrong is the initial step to choosing your crystal. For example, if you feel physical pain in a certain part of your body, this can be key to identifying which crystal would be the best one to treat you.

As an example, if you have been regularly experiencing an upset tummy or you suffer chronically from digestive system problems, then this is the condition that you want to treat. One stone that is often effective for helping to treat these kinds of conditions is the moonstone.

2. Choose your technique

You have already learned some practical techniques for using your crystals – including keeping them close to you to absorb the negative energy that can manifest as physical symptoms. You have also learned about visualisation and mindfulness techniques for easing mental and physical ailments. Later in the book, you will also learn more ways to use your crystals for healing.

Sometimes, it can be a good idea to experiment with various techniques as this will ensure that you find the right method for healing yourself, using your crystals. Some people find that wearing their crystal as an amulet works best for them.

Others prefer to use their crystals with yoga poses or to channel energy through their crystal during meditation practices. If you find that one method is not personally effective for you, switch to a different method until you identify the one that helps you.

3. Purify your stones

When you purchase new stones or even when you receive them as a gift, they may still have negative energy or other people's energy stored within them. Therefore, it is very important to cleanse them of any previous energy so that they can be optimised for your personal usage.

Later in the book, you will find a detailed guide to cleansing, purifying and recharging your stones. However, if you are simply looking for an easy way to prepare your stones, fill a small bowl with some uncooked grains of brown rice. Leave the stones in the bowl for one to two days before using them. Then, discard the rice and your crystals will be pure and ready to help you.

4. Harmonise the stones with your energy

Crystals should always be tuned so that they are in harmony with your own energy. You can think of this as helping the crystals to find your wavelength. In some ways, this is a little like tuning a radio station. Sit with your cleansed stones for a while and focus on the stone's vibrations. This will allow them to be set to your energy, tuning them perfectly and maximising their potential to draw out any negative energy from your body.

5. Focus on your health problem

No matter what kind of health problem you're suffering from – whether it is an emotional or physical ailment – visualising the issue while you set up your crystal is very important. Your mind is essentially using the crystal as a catalyst to drive forward the healing process and allow yourself to experience the maximum benefits of the crystal's potential to neutralise negative forces that are detrimentally affecting your body and mind.

Do not underestimate the power of your thoughts when it comes to using your crystals. Maintaining a strong focus to ensure that you open yourself to your crystal is very important and can be a key factor in allowing your crystals to work well.

Know Your Birthstones For Better Healing

Many crystal healers believe that some crystals are more effective depending on your birthday and zodiac sign. Your birthstone crystals might be more effective at helping you to heal than other crystals so, when you have a choice of multiple crystals that all share the same characteristics and healing properties, it can be beneficial to opt for your birthstone before anything else.

Birthstones

January – *Garnet* – the perfect stone for energising yourself and healing your physical body.

February – *Amethyst* – ideal for healing a disconnected spirit and detoxifying your blood.

March – *Aquamarine* – cleanses fear and worries when your mind is in turmoil whilst giving you a sense of serenity.

April – *Clear Quartz* (or *Diamond*) – lightens and refreshes your aura, helping you to recover from health problems and find good fortune.

May – *Emerald* – heals romantic trauma and promotes the healing and recovery of strained relationships.

June – *Moonstone* – excellent for moving on from regrets and allowing your psyche to heal and look forward, rather than backward.

July – *Ruby* – cleanses inhibitions that have been holding you back, allowing you to fulfil your dreams.

August – *Peridot* – perfect for purging suppressed and detrimental emotions that can cause anxiety, depression and other emotional issues.

September – *Sapphire* – cleanses your throat and third-eye chakras, opening you to the possibility of prosperity in all areas of your life, especially your confidence and creativity.

October – *Tourmaline* (or *Opal*) – rebalances and cleanses your chakras to treat physical and emotional issues.

November – *Citrine* – brings brightness into your life if you have endured depression or recent grief. It can also improve your general mood and help you to feel more ambitious.

December – *Turquoise* – grounds and centres your body when you feel spiritually and emotionally lost. Helps you to get in touch with your inner wisdom.

Zodiac Sign Stones

Aries – Bloodstone, Aventurine, Citrine, Jasper, Ruby, Chrysocolla

Taurus – Rose Quartz, Selenite, Lapis Lazuli, Agate, Aragonite, Rhodonite

Gemini – Moonstone, Garnet, Jet, Agate, Selenite, Citrine

Cancer – Emerald, Feldspar, Moonstone, Howlite, Tourmaline

Leo – Amber, Onyx, Sunstone, Peridot, Labradorite, Rhodonite

Virgo – Sapphire, Amazonite, Carnelian, Hawks Eye, Sardonyx, Charoite

Libra – Quartz, Lava, Moldavite, Tourmaline, Prehnite

Scorpio – Aventurine, Tourmaline, Malachite, Garnet, Obsidian, Hematite

Sagittarius – Turquoise, Fluorite, Sodalite, Tektite

Capricorn – Amber, Amethyst, Pyrite, Sodalite, Labradorite, Hypersthene

By using your birthstones or zodiac stones as your primary healing crystals or by placing them around your home, in your car and at your workplace, you can promote more effective healing, ward off negativity and maintain better peace of mind.

Even if you do not use them for meditative techniques, simply having them present in your close environment will help to channel their positive energy toward you and assist in cleansing your body due to their close proximity.

Cleanse Your Chakras

The concept of chakras comes from Ancient Indian culture and is recognised in modern alternative medicine. "Chakra" means "wheel" in Sanskrit. Your main chakras are the seven energy centres in your body and they correspond to specific organs and nerves.

Chakras must be clean, clear and unblocked to allow your energy to flow efficiently through your body, allowing you to function at your best. When a chakra becomes blocked, it can cause emotional and physical problems. This can lead to significant issues and if your seven main chakras are blocked, crystals can be used to help unblock them, allowing the energy to flow freely through them, healing and repairing the problems that a blockage has caused.

When a chakra becomes blocked, energy cannot pass through it in an effective way. For example, when your root chakra, which is associated with security and stability, becomes blocked, symptoms can manifest as insecurity, melancholy and even clinical depression.

Chakras can also be thrown out of balance and allow *too much* energy to flow through them. If a chakra is unbalanced and overactive, it can also have detrimental effects on your psyche. For example, when the root chakra is allowing too much energy to flow, you may experience recklessness or take unusual and eccentric steps to try and achieve a sense of security, such as hoarding behaviours.

Blocked or overactive chakras can lead to substantial emotional and physical health problems and these symptoms can manifest as a variety of conditions. In many cases, you will notice that your physical symptoms occur in the region of the chakra that is specifically blocked or unbalanced. Often, the muscles, organs, joints, bones and other tissues in that region will be affected. For example, if your crown chakra is blocked, this could lead to headaches.

When it comes to suffering from emotional symptoms due to a blocked or unbalanced chakra, this can be slightly more complicated because it is more difficult to identify which chakra has become unbalanced. If you experience symptoms like melancholy, indecision, fear and anger, this could relate to a number of chakras. Sometimes, you may need to work on each chakra, in turn, to cleanse it and release the energy so it can flow more freely.

Crystals are an excellent tool for helping to unblock your chakras. They can be used effectively alone or you can utilise them as part of a wider healing strategy. Later, we will look at some exercises, including breathing exercises, meditation and yoga postures that can be used alongside crystals to maximise your healing potential when you're using your crystals.

It is always essential to ensure that you use the correct kinds of crystals to unblock a specific chakra because different crystals relate better to the various energy centres in your body. Think of a crystal as a tool in a tool kit. You would not use a hammer to unscrew a bolt as it would not work. Similarly, you wouldn't use a spanner to put a nail into a wall. While all crystals have their own effectiveness, they should be used in the right way for your cleansing and healing to work properly.

Root Chakra

The Root Chakra, also known as the *Muladhara*, is the chakra that controls characteristics such as your sense of stability and security. As the name indicates, this chakra is located at the bottom of your spine.

This chakra is the first of the seven chakras. In many ways, the Root Chakra can be responsible for your sense of self. It is representative of your most basics desires and physical and emotional needs. It sets out the foundation for all the other chakras and the rest of your spirit and personality.

Red is the colour that is most associated with this chakra and red stones can often be used as a way to heal and cleanse this energy centre in your body.

When the Root Chakra becomes damaged or disconnected from nature, crystals can heal these problems, helping you to feel grounded and reconnect you to your sense of self again.

If your root chakra is blocked or unbalanced, several physical symptoms can manifest as a result. Some of the most common symptoms are:

- Colon issues

- Bladder problems

- Constipation

- Arthritis

Crystals

There is an array of crystals that support the root chakra:

Brown Jasper: Brown jasper is found in a variety of hues. It is perfect for strengthening your connections with nature and bringing you closer to the Earth's electromagnetic forces.

Red Jasper: Red jasper is linked with the fertility of the earth and was highly prized by the Ancient Egyptians for this reason. It symbolizes energy, life and physicality.

Mahogany Obsidian: A stone that is coloured with stunning stripes and sports, Mahogany Obsidian is a hybrid of Black Obsidian and Hematite. It can connect your body to the energy field of the earth as well as bringing your connection closer to others around you. It is perfect for providing a closer bond in relationships and boosting your confidence in others and yourself.

Onyx: Onyx is an excellent stone to be used to cleanse and strengthen the root chakra. It is best suited to boosting your physical responses and sharpening your senses. It is perfect for heightening your feeling of protection.

Garnet: Garnet harmonises with the root chakra's red hue and can allow you to feel heightened emotional stability. If you have felt lost or nomadic, this stone can give you an increased sense of emotional stability and belonging. What's more, garnet is perfect for healing emotional problems, especially within relationships. It also links with the other chakras to allow energy to flow freely throughout your body which helps to unblock any blockages.

Tourmaline: An ideal protector against negativity, Tourmaline acts as a shield against sinister forces. It can help you to feel grounded, secure and stable, cleansing your root chakra and removing any blockages.

Bloodstone: This is a stone that can help you to channel your physical energy through the healing power of the sun and the earth. It is an excellent source for boosting vitality and healing emotional and physical health problems.

Practice

- Take your crystals and place them into your hands.

- Focus on the crystal and visualize the deep red energy flowing through the crystal into your chakra.

- Use the affirmation - "I AM a strong, stable and secure person."

Sacral Chakra

Your Sacral Chakra or *Swadhisthana* is located just underneath your belly button and over your pelvic bone. It is the body's centre of creativity, pleasure and sensuality.

Orange is often associated with this chakra and, when using visualisation techniques, this can be an excellent colour on which to focus.

In an emotional sense, the sacral chakra is connected with feelings of sexuality and creativity. It is one of the body's pleasure centres and blockages can lead to impeded self-worth, lack of creativity and low mood. A blocked sacral chakra can cause low motivation and difficulty in finding pleasure in daily activities.

What's more, you may experience difficulty in establishing deep, intimate and affectionate emotional connections with other people when your sacral chakra is in trouble. Even your appreciation for simple pleasures, such as good food or fine wines can be damaged. Therefore, you may notice that you experience a poor appetite and low libido.

Physically, many problems can arise when this chakra is not in balance or energy is not able to freely flow through it. The symptoms include:

- Pain in the lower back

- Reproductive issues

- Impotency

- Frequent urinary tract or bladder infections

Crystals

Orange Calcite: Orange calcite is a crystal that harmonises with the sacral chakra, thanks to its rich orange colour. It is an energising crystal that cleanses and refreshes this energy centre, ensuring that negative energy is purged from your sacral chakra and blockages are efficiently dealt with.

Carnelian: The name of this sun comes from the Ancient Egyptian term for a sun that is setting. This is because the colouration of the stone resembles the sun as it dips below the horizon. Associated with reproduction and fertility, carnelian can be used to treat reproductive issues such as conception struggles and impotence. It is excellent for boosting desire.

Sunstone: If you experience physical problems in this area, such as UTI or bladder infections, sunstone is an excellent healing tool to help stimulate your body's natural restorative capabilities. This stone is naturally connected to the sun's natural energy field and channels this energy to rebalance your sacral chakra when you experience health issues that are connected to the area.

Snowflake Obsidian: An extremely grounding stone, snowflake obsidian is ideal for rebalancing your sacral chakra. When your energy is blocked, this stone can be used to free the blockage and reset the chakra to its natural and healthy state.

Peach Aventurine: Peach Aventurine, also known as the whispering stone, can settle the mind when the sacral chakra is inflamed and imbalanced. If you have experienced guilt connected to pleasures, especially sensual pleasures, this crystal can be used to help silence that guilt and cleanse yourself of the negative feelings that can be associated with guilt.

Unakite: This stone is a blend of Epidote and Red Jasper. It is often used to establish healthy and happy relationships, increase intimacy in relationships and cleanse your mind of past traumas connected to love and affection.

- Take your crystals and hold them in your hands.

- Focus on the crystal and visualize the orange energy flowing through the crystal into your chakra.

- Use the affirmation - "I FEEL creative, open and sociable."

Solar Plexus Chakra

The third chakra is your Solar Plexus Chakra (*Manipura)* and it is located just beneath your sternum (breastbone). It is the centre of confidence and the notion of "self." This chakra is important for maintaining the balance of creating your boundaries and allowing yourself to experience pleasure. In this chakra, you will find your self-confidence and resilience.

This chakra is associated with the colour yellow and often works well for cleansing and balancing with yellow-hued stones. When the solar plexus is functioning correctly, you will notice that you experience strong motivation, passion and endurance.

When the solar plexus chakra is out of balance or blocked, it can lead to substantial physical and mental health problems. You may observe that you feel tired, frail, weak and lack motivation. You might also have problems with your gut and liver.

Emotionally, the effects can be extremely severe and detrimental if your solar plexus is suffering from an imbalance. Common symptoms include a sensation of worthlessness, a lack of mental direction and low levels of self-esteem. Guilt and a general disinterest in life can also manifest when your solar plexus needs to be cleansed.

Crystals

Citrine: With its lustrous yellow colour and harmonious energy, citrine is the ideal stone for cleansing your solar plexus chakra and healing the elements associated with an imbalance in this energy centre. It can remove the negative vibrations, clear a blockage and boost your confidence and self-esteem. Citrine is an excellent stone for restoring your feeling of power over your life and refocusing your direction.

Calcite: This orangey-lemon coloured stone amplifies your positive energy and reflects it back to you, ensuring that you maintain a good state of mental and physical wellbeing. It is perfect for using to practise yoga, especially during sun salutations.

Amber: With its fiery tones and energetic vibrations, Amber is excellent for rebalancing your energy in the solar plexus. It can channel the energy of sunlight, helping to purify your body and heal physical ailments. Additionally, it is good for achieving a greater state of clarity and helping you to make important decisions.

Pyrite: To restore your drive when you're experiencing a lack of motivation, try Pyrite. It is excellent for eliminating sluggishness and fatigue and restoring your lost vitality.

Tiger's Eye: Tiger's eye is a stone often used for unleashing you from fearfulness and allowing you to live your best life. If you have noticed that you feel directionless or mired in confusion, this stone can unshackle you from those tethers and boost your confidence to pursue your ambitions.

Yellow Topaz: Yellow Topaz is cleansing and therefore, perfect for physical detoxes. It washes away the blockages in your system and works well for helping to heal physical ailments when used during meditation.

Yellow Jasper: A protective stone, Yellow Jasper can absorb negative energy and purify your solar plexus chakra. This makes it a deeply healing stone when you're experiencing some of the negative health symptoms that are linked to malfunctions of the solar plexus chakra.

Yellow Tourmaline: This is a stone that quickly draws negative vibes out of your body whilst simultaneously stimulating your motivation so you will find that your confidence and drive increase.

Agate: If your passion has been manifesting as anger rather than motivation recently, your solar plexus can be cleansed, purified and rebalanced with the use of this volcanic stone. It can help you to rid yourself of previous negative energies and restore a positive balance in your third chakra.

Sunstone: Sunstone is a crystal that is ideally suited to boosting your positivity, increasing your confidence and self-esteem, stimulating your intellect and providing you with the mental space to enjoy emotional clarity.

Yellow Quartz: A clogged third chakra can lead to the development of negative thought cycles. This stone is perfect for breaking those cycles and drawing your worries out of your body. Consequently, your mind will be freer to concentrate on positive pursuits.

Practice

- Take your crystals and hold them in your hands.

- Focus on the crystal and visualize the yellow energy flowing through the crystal into your chakra.

- Use the affirmation - "I DO have strength, motivation, determination and power."

Heart Chakra

The fourth chakra, also known as the Heart Chakra or *Anahata,* is the seat of your emotional energy. It is generally linked with the colours green and pink. This is a crucial energy centre for your empathy, trust, compassion and self-love. It is also the centre of your ability to connect intimately with other people.

The Heart Chakra bridges the gap between the lower chakras, which tend to be grounding and the higher chakras which are spiritual.

When this chakra functions well, you will notice that you have a strong sense of self-care and the capability to care for other people. You will also be able to forgive the mistakes of others and move on from previous bad experiences. If your Heart Chakra is clear and working as it is supposed to work, you can gladly experience the best parts of life.

However, when this chakra misfires it can be extremely detrimental and damaging to your emotions. You can experience depression, anxiety and loneliness. Additionally, you may lack a sense of belonging and feel lost and out of place. Jealousy, lack of trust and unfair judgements are also linked with an unbalanced or blocked Heart Chakra.

Many physical symptoms can also arise when there are problems in this chakra. For example, you can experience heart problems, palpitations, irregular blood pressure, bad circulation and difficulties with your breathing.

Crystals

Rose Quartz: A crystal that is related to your ability to give and receive unconditional love, Rose Quartz is ideal for healing the heart in an emotional and physical sense. It can also help you to feel more compassion for yourself and boost your ability to practise self-care.

Green Aventurine: This dark green stone can absorb your negative energies in the heart chakra, giving you a sense of lightness. It is a great healer and suited to helping you achieve harmony and peace with your inner self. It also opens your heart so that you are able to attract new loves and connections as well giving you the courage to act on opportunities when they arise.

Emerald: To bring your heart chakra back into the right balance, discover a sense of inner harmony and find trust in yourself, emerald is the ideal stone. When you have experienced heartache that has left lasting scars, emerald can help you to heal, even from past traumas. It allows you to find wisdom and helps you to trust your own intuition.

Amazonite: This stone helps to bridge the gap between your heart chakra and your throat chakra. Therefore, when the cleansing energy rebalances these chakras, you will notice that not only are you able to feel love and trust more easily, but you will also enjoy the confidence to express these emotions much more freely.

Malachite: Like Amazonite, Malachite heightens your ability to express your feelings. It is also useful for protecting you against absorbing too much energy for those around you. Therefore, if you are an empathic person and you notice your moods are easily affected by the moods of others, it is a good idea to wear an item of jewellery, such as an amulet, that can offer you some protection from being overwhelmed by other people's emotions.

Green Calcite: Green calcite can rid you of frustration and remove the negative energies that can manifest as physical symptoms like high blood pressure and breathing difficulties. It brings a sense of peace to your heart and heals emotional wounds, even if they are old scars.

Rhodonite: Excellent at balancing the heart chakra, this stone reforms the foundations that give you the stability to experience love, trust and compassion for others. It is useful for times when you have experienced trauma and grief as these emotions can unbalance the heart chakra.

Practice

- Take your crystals and hold them in your hands.

- Focus on the crystal and visualize the green energy flowing through the crystal into your chakra.

- Use the affirmation - "I LOVE myself, accept myself, feel compassion and appreciate others."

Throat Chakra

Your Throat Chakra (*Vishuddha)* is the seat of your communication, honesty, expression, creativity and emotion. It is associated with the colour blue so blue-hued crystals are often used to cleanse and restore this chakra.

When your Throat Chakra becomes blocked or there is an imbalance in it, you can often experience symptoms such as communication problems and a lack of inspiration or creativity. Essentially, you might struggle to express yourself effectively and find that there are frequent miscommunications and misunderstandings.

As well as the spiritual and emotional symptoms, you might also find that you suffer from physical effects like a sore throat, problems with your hearing and an overactive or underactive thyroid.

Using crystals, you can unblock this chakra, encourage the energy to flow freely through it and realign your energy centre so that it functions correctly.

Crystals

Lapis Lazuli: This gem is ideally suited to helping you enhance your creativity and express yourself clearly. It can also be used to heal rifts in relationships and friendships by promoting more open lines of communication.

Turquoise: Turquoise is an extremely protective stone that can heal damaged self-esteem and restore your confidence when you're expressing yourself. What's more, this stone is excellent for encouraging the free flow of energy through all your chakras, allowing you to bridge the gap between each chakra and enjoy heightened creativity and wholeness.

Amazonite: This stone works by calming your nervous system and cleansing your throat chakra of negative energy that might have resulted in a blockage. It can restore your emotional balance and lay solid foundations to boost your confidence and self-esteem.

Aquamarine: This crystal is very skilled for cleansing your throat chakra and opening it. It simulates energy to flow liberally through this chakra and ensures that you can communicate honestly, expressing yourself effectively. It can give you clarity of speech, meaning that others will freely understand your message.

Angelite: For treating and healing physical symptoms that originate in the throat chakra, such as thyroid problems, Angelite can be a restorative stone. Additionally, it is perfect for helping to unblock emotional imbalances and allows you to feel increased compassion and speak truthfully.

Practice

- Take your crystals and hold them in your hands.

- Focus on the crystal and visualize the turquoise energy flowing through the crystal into your chakra.

- Use the affirmation - "I TALK well. I can express myself and communicate effectively to inspire others."

Third Eye Chakra

The Third Eye Chakra (*Ajna*) is the sixth of the seven primary chakras. It is located at the top of your nose, between your eyebrows. This energy centre is responsible for managing intellect, intuition and insight. It is the seat of your inspiration and spiritual connections. Purple and indigo are the colours that are most associated with the Third Eye Chakra.

The sixth chakra can determine characteristics such as wisdom, perception, imagination and spiritual vision. When it is working well, you can experience profound creativity, deep insight and a sense of feeling psychically connected to others.

However, a blocked Third Eye Chakra can manifest in multiple ways. Emotionally, you may notice that you are constantly fearful with a sense of foreboding. You will not be able to think outside the box but will instead be limited by your consciousness. Your imagination will be stunted and you might lack direction and clarity. Additionally, you will find that you struggle with introspectiveness or self-awareness. A blocked sixth chakra can also lead to insomnia, paranoia and oversensitivity in the face of criticism.

When it comes to your physical wellbeing, you may experience several various symptoms if your Third Eye Chakra is not balanced or if there is an energy blockage in this area. Some of these symptoms may include nightmares, headaches, low mood, imbalances in your hormone levels, sinus pain, fatigue, eye problems and clumsiness.

Placing a healing crystal over your third eye, between your eyebrows, can start to draw out the negative energy from this chakra, unblocking it and rebalancing it.

Crystals

Amethyst: Amethyst is an excellent treatment to combat recurrent nightmares and improve your self-awareness. If you are struggling with direction, clarity and decision making, this stone can help to clear your mind and allow you to gain better insight into your situation.

Labradorite: If you have been suffering from a lack of imagination and feel that your intellect has been stunted by brain fog, Labradorite is ideal for clearing the mind and stimulating your intuition. It can help to heal problems with the brain and eyes too.

Sodalite: Sodalite is perfect for helping to restore your intuition and give you better clarity. It can shatter negative thought patterns and anxiety, restore your emotional balance and improve your mood.

Blue Quartz: This stone is very effective for healing both your physical symptoms and your emotional symptoms. Physically, it can help with eye disorders and hormone imbalances. Emotionally, you can achieve a sense of peacefulness, improved clarity and better concentration levels once your chakra has been cleansed using the Blue Quartz.

Ametrine: A very effective treatment for healing all kinds of headaches, Ametrine is a blend of Citrine and Amethyst. It can help you to open your mind to new experiences and gain a higher level of consciousness.

Practice

- Take your crystals and hold them in your hands.

- Focus on the crystal and visualize the blue energy flowing through the crystal into your chakra.

- Use the affirmation - "I SEE everything. I trust my own intuition and have the ability to trust in others."

Crown Chakra

The Crown Chakra (*Sahasrara*) is the seventh and final chakra of the seven main chakras. This chakra is linked to a sense of unity and higher consciousness. It can allow you to sense the purpose of your life. The colour generally associated with the Crown Chakra is violet. It is the most spiritual and esoteric of all the chakras. It is found at your head's crown.

When this chakra becomes unbalanced, it can make you feel cynical, jaded, depressed, irresponsible, lonely and ungrounded. Physically, a blocked crown chakra can result in headaches, dizziness and numbness or tingling in the head area, especially at the top of your head or around your temples.

Crystals

Selenite: Selenite is an essential crystal in restoring the crown chakra and opening your mind. It can improve your insight, help you to discover your life's purpose and boost your positivity.

Lepidolite: Ideal for both physical healing and mental wellbeing, this stone allows you to purge fear from your mind and achieve better clarity. It will balance your energy, paving the way for you to experience deeper levels of happiness.

Sugilite: This stone is perfect for establishing a connection between your crown chakra and your heart chakra, ensuring that energy flows freely between the two. It can allow you to move forward if you have endured traumas and embrace forgiveness.

Fluorite: Fluorite can help you to rebalance yourself and achieve a more open state of mind. It is excellent at dispelling confusion and cynicism.

Practice

- Take your crystals and hold them in your hands.

- Focus on the crystal and visualize the purple energy flowing through the crystal into your chakra.

- Use the affirmation - "I UNDERSTAND on a conscious and spiritual level."

Which Crystals Are Best For Healing Damaged Chakras?

In truth, most crystals are cleansing and healing to some extent. Crystals channel positive energy into your body whilst simultaneously absorbing negative energy and removing it from your body. As a result, you will find that you can use almost all your crystals to cleanse yourself.

Saying that, some crystals are particularly powerful when it comes to cleansing your chakras. As you read in the last chapter, many stones are associated with each chakra and each of these can be used for different cleansing and healing purposes. However, this easy-to-read guide will show you the best crystals to use when you require a quickfire and all-purpose cleansing.

First chakra – Black obsidian

To feel grounded, cleansed and revitalised, place your black obsidian crystal onto your bedside table or under your pillowcase at night. This can cleanse you of the stress of the day and help you to enjoy a natural, refreshing night's sleep.

Second chakra – Carnelian

For ladies who are experiencing menstrual cramps, place the carnelian stone onto your abdomen and lie down for an hour before bed. The stone can help to relieve the pain and emotional and hormonal stress that are associated with this time of the month.

For the gentlemen – if you are experiencing low libido, slip the stone into the pocket of your pyjama bottoms at night and remove it in the morning. Repeat this every night for a few weeks until you start to notice an improvement.

Third chakra – Citrine

If you're lacking in creativity and in need of a boost to your self-confidence, you can cleanse your negative energy and unblock your third chakra with citrine. To inspire yourself, wrap a citrine crystal in a banknote and carry it in your pocket. This can help to unblock your ambition and prosperity and cleanse any bad luck you've had in business.

Fourth chakra – Rose Quartz

To heal from trauma in love and cleanse yourself of past toxic relationships, start by purifying your rose quartz crystal by wafting it in the smoke of burning sage. Place the crystal into a bowl of river water, seawater or purified water. Set the bowl outside in the sunlight for an entire day (from sunrise to sunset.)

Remove the crystal from the bowl and pay it dry. Then, pour the water from the bowl into an empty spray bottle. To the bottle add 44 drops of almond oil and 22 drops of rose oil. Shake the mixture and screw on the cap of the bottle. Use it as a cleansing spray every morning and evening. Keep the crystal in a breast pocket so it is close to your heart.

This dual method of cleansing is particularly effective for ensuring that your fourth chakra is fully cleansed and your mind is opened to new possibilities of love.

Fifth chakra – Lapis Lazuli

If you are worried about speaking in public, give yourself a lapis lazuli cleanse beforehand. Hold the stone in your non-dominant hand and recite affirmations such as:

"I'm a confident speaker."

"My speech will go well."

"I can communicate with ease and grace."

"I know my material extensively and comprehensively."

Perform this activity every morning for a week before you are due to speak in public and it will cleanse away any fear, negativity and reticence that may be associated with public speaking.

Sixth and seventh chakras – Amethyst

If you are battling with a hangover, place your amethyst crystals onto your forehead and lie down in a darkened room for an hour. Visualise a cleansing white light emanating from the stone and cascading down through your head, neutralising your pain and rejuvenating you.

For anyone who is detoxing, amethyst can be carried at all times to maintain sobriety and ward off the temptation to indulge in a tipple.

Recharging And Cleansing Your Crystals

Crystals help you to channel the natural energy that flows from sources such as the sun, earth and water. However, when they are used regularly, they need to be purified and recharged so that their efficiency can be optimised. If you don't cleanse them, it is like endlessly reusing a coffee filter or a tea strainer and never rinsing them out. They might still work to some extent but their full potential will be compromised.

So, how can you easily recharge and purify your crystals?

Well, it is actually a relatively easy process and there are many ways in which to do so:

Natural sunlight and moonlight

Recharge your crystals in natural sunlight or moonlight – crystals often take their healing power from solar or lunar light so one of the best ways to recharge them is to set them under the natural light and allow the light sources to bathe them. Stones tend to also draw energy from the earth too. As a result, the best idea is to place them outside on the ground for 12 hours, either in daylight or moonlight.

This method works well for the majority of tumbled stones. However, some stones should be kept out of direct sunlight. Amethyst and other vibrant crystals can be damaged if they are left in sunlight. Vibrant stones can be recharged and cleansed using some of the other methods below. Softer stones, like halite, celestite and selenite may also not be suitable for recharging outside as they can be easily damaged in adverse weather conditions.

Freshwater purification

Fresh running water helps to neutralise the negative energy that can build up a stone, especially when that crystal has been regularly used for cleansing the energy from your chakras or for unblocking them. The best kind of water to use in this method of purification is to take your crystals to a river, stream or brook.

You can use any source of natural running water and this will wash away the negative energy. For it to be fully effective, submerge your stone entirely under the running water for around one minute and then carefully pat the crystal dry when the cleansing is complete.

Of course, not everybody has easy access to these kinds of water sources, especially if you live in an urban area. So, you can also run your stone under tap water to cleanse and re-energise them.

Freshwater purification works best for harder stones like quartz but should be avoided for more brittle stones like halite and selenite.

Saltwater cleansing

Salt is an ancient and natural purification tool that has been used throughout human history to help remove negative energy from various sources.

In this method, you can use a natural salt source, such as seawater or ocean water. However, if you don't live near to this kind of saltwater source and cannot gain access to it, you can mix water with packaged salts. When you choose your salt, try and opt for naturally sourced salt, like sea salt or rock salts and mix it together with tap water in a bowl.

Once you have your water, place the stones into the water and leave them to soak for 36-46 hours. The salt will draw the energy out of the stones, cleansing them and allowing them to recharge themselves so they will be fully optimised for their next use.

It is important to avoid using this method with porous stones, like malachite, calcite and halite. Saltwater cleansing works best with stones like quartz, amethyst and other hard crystals.

Brown rice cleansing

Brown rice is a substance that is excellent for drawing the negativity out of your stones and recharging stones that have a protective energy field, like tourmaline. If you have ever dropped your mobile phone into water, brown rice can be used to soak up the water. This method works on the same principle – except that the rice soaks up the bad energy rather than water. Always use uncooked grains of rice for this purification ritual.

It is very easy and relatively quick to use this method. Simply pour some brown rice into a bowl and bury the crystals underneath the rice. Leave the bowl of rice for around 24 hours to allow it to fully draw all the negative energy from the stones. Once you have finished, remove the stones and discard the rice. Do not consume the rice that you used as it will have soaked up all the bad energy and you do not want to ingest this.

One of the best things about cleansing your stones with brown rice is that it works on all stones and crystals without exception. It will not harm or damage your stones so it can also be used on soft, brittle and porous crystals too.

Sage purification and recharging

Sage is an ancient, sacred plant that has been associated with healing throughout history. Sage is often burned to cleanse the environment around you and it can be used in a similar manner to cleanse your stones of any negative energy they may have absorbed. It is excellent for restoring the natural, vibrant energy of a stone and making it harmonious again.

It is best to conduct this ritual outside or close to an open door or window so that the negative energy can efficiently flow away. Take your sage and place it into a heatproof bowl before igniting the tip of the plant. Waft the crystal that you wish to cleanse through the smoke generated by the burning sage.

Leave the stone in the smoke for around a minute, giving the sage smoke some time to fully wash away all the energy that has built up in the stone. This is especially important if you have not cleansed your stones in a while because an increased amount of negative energy will have built up within them.

Sage purification can be used will all stones and crystals and has the dual effect of drawing bad energy away from the stone whilst also cleansing the environment around you. Therefore, if you feel you are surrounded by a large volume of negative energy, this can be an excellent multipurpose cleansing method.

Use other stones

Crystals and tumbled stones can actually be cleansed using other stones. Generally, it's important to choose a stone that is significantly larger or smaller than the stone you wish to cleanse.

If you are choosing a stone that is larger than your crystal, opt for stones such as amethyst geodes, slabs or selenite or quartz. You can purchase special "cleansing bowls" for this purpose. It is very simple and only entails placing your stone onto the larger stones and leaving them in a safe, cool, dry place for 24 hours. The larger stone will draw out the inharmonious energy from your stone, leaving it purified and recharged, ready for use.

When you choose smaller stones than your own stone for cleansing, you will need a handful of the smaller stones. Put the smaller stones into a bowl and place your stone on the top. Hematite and carnelian are perfect cleansing stones. As with the method for using larger stones, leave the stones to do their clearing work for around 24 hours. Ensure that the stones remain cool, dry and out of the sunlight while they cleanse your stone.

Both of these ways of cleansing can be used with all crystals and they are very effective. They work by drawing the negative energy out of your crystal. This is the same way that your crystals draw negative energy from your body.

If you wish to reuse your smaller or larger stones once you have finished the purification ritual, you can use one of the other methods in this book to cleanse them, such as brown rice purification. By doing so, you can reuse them at a later time to cleanse your stone again.

Sound Cleansing

Sound cleansing is one of the fastest methods of crystal purification, so it's excellent to use if you're in a hurry. The sound that you use should be loud, harmonious and clear, such as that of a bell or a tuning fork.

Ensure that the sound is emitted for around 10 minutes as this will fully cleanse the crystals. It is a versatile method and suitable for all crystals. If your crystal collection is extensive, this is a great way to cleanse all your stones simultaneously without having to move them or work through them all one by one.

To use sound cleansing, simply strike a bell or use a tuning fork for 10 minutes. This will recalibrate the crystals and restore their balance and harmony.

Breath purification

Human breath is a reliable and effective method of purification that is excellent for fast cleansing. It should be used with a single stone for each cleansing and works on all stones.

Begin by holding your stone in the hand that you use to write (i.e. your dominant hand.) If you are ambidextrous, use the hand that you tend to favour most of the time. Clear your mind and focus on your objective of cleansing the stone. Breath in through your nose and out through your mouth, setting a breath rhythm that you will use to cleanse the stone.

Hold it up in front of your face and breathe over the stone, essentially channelling your energy to remove any negative energy that has built up and been stored in the stone. Repeat this method for around one minute per stone.

The visualisation method

Visualisation is an excellent way to cleanse your crystals but it can take some practice before you really get the hang of it. Essentially, it works on the basis of being in harmony with your inner self so that you can channel your energy through your thoughts to purify your crystals.

Start by spending several minutes tuning yourself to the energy inside you. Think of your energy as a tangible substance, such a white light. When you have cemented the image in your mind, place your stone in your hands and visualise the white light flowing from your mind to the stones. Imagine the light fully enveloping the stone and brightening as it works on the stone.

Once the light is extremely bright and completely surrounds the stone, visualise all the impurities in the stone and imagine the light washing them all away. Finally, when the stone is cleansed of impurities and negative energy, visualise the light growing even brighter. This is the recharging portion of the method and will imbue the stone with positive energy.

Toward the end of the cleansing ritual, you will sense that the energy in your stone has transformed, signalling that the purification and renewal are complete.

You can use visualisation with any stone, but it can sometimes take a few tries before you become adept at using this method. Persevere, even if you find it daunting or you struggle at the start. It is extremely safe and a very effective way of renewing your crystals, so it's great to get the hang of it.

Why Is Crystal Cleansing A Necessity?

Caring for your crystals is the best way to keep them in good condition and ensure that they are at an optimal level for helping you to heal. If you neglect your crystals and do not cleanse them, they can become heavy and blocked by negative energy. Essentially, they will just stop working and you will not benefit from their healing effects anymore.

Many crystal enthusiasts often wonder how often they should cleanse their crystals. However, there is no hard and fast rule to dictate this. It all depends on the extent to which you use your crystals. The more that you utilise your crystals, the more negative energy will be collected inside your stone. Therefore, if you use your stones frequently, you should cleanse and purify them more regularly than if you are simply an occasional user.

However, even if you only use your crystals for cleansing from time to time, it is important to remember that crystals can also absorb some negative energy from the environment around you. Consequently, even if you rarely use some of the crystals in your collection, you should try to ensure that you cleanse *all* of them at least once every month.

Sometimes, when you pick up a certain stone, you will notice that it feels heavy and dark. This can be a strong indication that it needs to be cleansed. Even if you have purified it recently, some stones can quickly become blocked again. As time goes on, you will get to know your stones and have a feel for how often they require purification.

As you have read, there are many different methods of purifying your stones. Different methods often work better for different people. Therefore, if you are new to crystal healing, it's essential to experiment with the different types of purification to identify which method is the most suitable one for you and your crystals.

Cleansing can take time and effort to perfect. Over time, you will become practised at learning when your crystal has been cleansed because it will feel lighter and more vibrant following a cleansing. As you become harmonised and more in tune with your stones, you will gain a sense of when they are purified and recharged.

Post-purification, you should also find the ideal place to store your crystals when they are not in use. Remember that stones are natural and they flourish most effectively when they are kept in natural settings. For example, if you have a houseplant in your home, crystals can benefit from being kept in close proximity to the plant. Storing your stones close to a window – although out of direct sunlight – can also be beneficial to them. Ultimately, try and keep them as close to nature as you can. They were formed in nature and this is a great way to keep them bursting full of natural energy that you can use to heal yourself.

Crystal Programming

When your stone has been cleansed and purified, it is important to programme it so it is in tune with you and so that you are in tune with the frequency of the crystal's energy. It is very simple to connect your energy to that of the stones.

All you need to do is follow these steps:

- Place the stone in your hand and allow yourself to feel the vibrations and warmth that are emitted by the crystal.

- Visualise the energy that is radiating from the crystal. Picture the colour of the light that represents the energy.

- Take a deep breath and focus on your own inner energy. Picture your energy and your crystal's energy merging.

- Communicate with your stone and ask it to help you with the objective that you wish to achieve.

- Show your gratitude to the crystal by thanking it for its help.

- Retain the stone in your hand and practise some meditation techniques.

Once your crystal has been programmed, it should need to be reprogrammed until after you have cleansed and purified it again. It will stay connected with you and ensure that it absorbs any negative energy from you, even when you are not actively using it.

Crystal Activation

Activating, or reactivating your crystal may be necessary when it starts to lose its shine or feels heavier than it normally does. By interacting with your crystal through speech, song or breathing on it, you can give it an energy boost and revitalise it.

You can also help your stone to activate by taking it out into nature. Remember that these stones are formed from natural materials and so the outdoors is the most comfortable habitat. Take the stone to a watery area such as a beach or a riverbank or take it to a green and grassy area like a park or the woods.

Another method of activating your stone is to surround it with other stones that are rich in energy. Some of these energy-rich stones include:

- Selenite

- Ruby

- Clear Quartz

- Carnelian

Once you have activated your stone, you will notice that it feels lighter, seems to hum and vibrate with energy and has a shinier and more lustrous appearance. Once you see this, you will know that your stone's energy levels have been restored and it is ready for use again.

Crystal Meditation

Meditation provides a myriad of benefits for its proponents. For centuries, meditative practices have been common in Eastern countries and an integral part of many religions. In more recent decades, they have become integrated into popular cultures. Now, there are many proven scientific benefits to meditation.

For example:

Lower stress levels: Studies have shown that meditation can reduce levels of stress, calm the mind and benefit your physical and emotional wellbeing.

Better quality of sleep: Not only does meditation promote healthier sleep schedules but it can also ensure that you achieve longer periods of deep sleep, leaving you feeling rejuvenated and refreshed in the mornings.

Lower blood pressure: As meditation helps you to relax, it can slow your heartbeat and lower your blood pressure.

Break addictive and negative cycles: Meditation is excellent at helping you to focus your mind, avoid addictive behaviours and distracts you from self-destructive behaviours.

Using crystals when you meditate can enhance the overall efficacy of your mediation practise and ensure that you cleanse your body and focus your energy. This can stimulate your body to heal and repair and restore fragmentations in your mental health and emotional state.

Practices

Crystal circle

When you perform your mediations, you can surround yourself with a circle of crystals and sit cross-legged in the middle. You can also place the crystals around your chair, bed or anywhere else you are meditating.

When you form a crystal circle, you can use more than one variety of crystal but it is important not to use too many types as the energy can become overly confused if you do.

Once you have prepared the circle, you can choose to use a guided mediation, listen to calm and relaxing music or sounds of nature or practice a yoga meditation routine.

The crystals will enhance the positive energy and calmness that you generate during the meditation whilst simultaneously drawing any bad vibes away from you.

Bath meditation

- Run a hot bath. You can add bubble bath or relaxing essential oils such as lavender and sandalwood to the bathwater.

- Place a crystal on the side of the bath or hold it in your hand when you are in the water. Avoid using porous crystals when you are practising these bath time meditations as they may dissolve in the water.

- Close your eyes and focus on the crystal in your hand. Pay attention to the feel of the water and its heat. Listen to the sound of your breath.

- Breathe in and count to four. Hold the breath for four beats. Exhale your breath and count to four. Hold for a further four beats. Repeat the cycle several times until you notice a sense of calm coming over you.

Crystal Breathwork

Breathing exercises are excellent for helping your crystals to cleanse your negative energy and heal you. In this section, we will explore some of the various exercises that you can use for healing.

When you perform breathwork in combination with crystals, you should focus on both your breath and the healing energy of the crystals.

Cleansing breathing

When you are feeling that your energy is blocked, you may notice a mental fog. Your focus and concentration can be disturbed. If this is the case, using a tandem combination of crystals and cleansing breaths is the ideal way to clear out any blockages and ensure that you rebalance your internal energy.

For this exercise, choose crystals such as:

- Clear quartz
- Ruby
- Carnelian

- Apophyllite

1. Cup your crystal in your dominant hand (your preferred writing hand) and focus on the crystal.

2. Visualise the crystal's energy field as a bright white light. Concentrate on the light.

3. Place your non-dominant hand over one nostril and close your nostril.

4. Breathe in slowly but, rather than inhaling *air* alone, visualise inhaling the white light from the crystal's energy field too.

5. Once you have fully inhaled the light, hold your breath. Remove your hand from your nostril and shut off the other nostril instead.

6. Exhale gradually and smoothly and visualise black light leaving your body during your exhaling breath.

7. Repeat the exercise until the light that you exhale is also white. This will signal that all the darkness and negative energy has been removed and

cleaned from your body, leaving you with a much cleaner energy field.

8. Remember to purify your crystal after this exercise because it will be extremely heavy with negative energy so it will require a good recharge.

Energising breathing

Lethargy is something that can affect many people and there might be a variety of reasons why you are suffering from fatigue. It can be caused by overwork, lack of sleep or even various stresses and strains that occur in the course of normal life.

If you feel lethargic, then channelling energy through your crystals, as you practise breathwork, can intensify the efficacy of your breathing exercises and improve your symptoms. You may notice improvements such as increased energy levels, better focus and less sluggishness.

For this exercise, you will need to use crystals that are energising and can boost your mental focus and energy levels.

These include:

- Citrine

- Amethyst

- Rose Quartz

- Lapis Lazuli

- Black Obsidian

1. Take your choice of crystal in your hands and focus on the crystal, allowing your energy to harmonise with the crystal's energy.

2. Breathe in rapidly through your nose in a sharp and short beat. Then, without exhaling take another more gradual breath.

3. Immediately, without holding the breath, exhale quickly with a short breath. Follow that instantly with a longer exhale.

4. Repeat this cycle five times.

5. Take a two-minute break and then repeat the exercise.

This exercise allows the crystal to amplify the energising effects of your breath whilst simultaneously cleansing any negative energy that is slowing you down or making you feel fatigued.

You can try this breathing technique at any time and anywhere. It is particularly effective when you really require a swift burst of energy, such as before exams or job interviews.

Calming breathing

Anxiety, stress and worry are conditions that affect most of us at some point in our lives. Life can be extremely stressful, with a large percentage of the population attempting to juggle multiple responsibilities at the same time.

Modern life is busier than ever, so this calming breathing exercise can help to heal your anxiety and calm your stress by using the healing energy of the crystal you use.

Some of the best, most appropriate crystals for performing this exercise are:

- Black tourmaline

- Blue lace agate

- Angelite

- Fluorite

- Celestite

1. Take a seated position but ensure that you are not reclining or lying down.

2. Take your crystal in your dominant hand – i.e. the hand that you use for writing.

3. Inhale deeply through your nose for five seconds.

4. Hold your breath for six seconds.

5. Purse your lips and then breathe out forcefully through your mouth, counting to seven as you do so.

6. Hold for eight seconds before you repeat.

Yoga Poses And Crystals

Yoga is an ancient art that is now practised across the world. In recent years, yoga has become exceptionally popular thanks to its benefits for fitness and centring the mind.

Yoga offers benefits such as increasing your strength, helping to boost bone density, relaxing your mind, lowering your blood pressure,

Whether you are motivated to boost your fitness levels, focus your mind, increase your flexibility or ground yourself, using crystals to improve the efficacy of your yoga practice is an excellent strategy for maximising your potential.

Types Of Yoga

There are countless different styles of yoga, with some being old, traditional styles while other types are more modern and have been developed more recently. It is important to find a yoga style that suits you because you may require a slower or faster style to achieve your objectives.

It's important to remember that you are not limited to practising a single style of yoga. In fact, you can practise multiple types of yoga, tailoring them to your needs. For example, if you are in need of healing for your anxiety or low mood, you may want to practice one form of yoga, such as Hatha yoga. A few weeks later, you may feel that you are heavy with negative energy and be embarking on a physical detox from sugar or alcohol. In that case, Bikram yoga would be more appropriate.

Hatha yoga: This is one of the gentlest classes of yoga and is perfect for meditative yoga practice. It is ideally suited to use with crystals for relaxation, lessening stress and healing low moods and negative thought cycles.

Ashtanga yoga: This is significantly more energetic and vigorous than some other forms of yoga. It follows a quick pace of various salutations and poses. For anyone who is suffering from low energy levels, pair ashtanga yoga practice with the use of crystals that promote increased energy flow.

Bikram yoga: If your energy centres are blocked, this form of yoga is perfect for helping to cleanse you of toxins and negative energy. When your energy centres are impeded, you might experience symptoms like a lack of creativity, low motivation and conflict in your relationships and friendships. Bikram yoga used heat to purge your body of physical toxins. In the same way, pairing this practice with the use of crystals can draw our impure and inharmonious energies from your body, mind and chakras.

Yin yoga: This form of yoga is good for anyone who feels overworked and suffers from aching joints or a lack of flexibility – which can also include emotional flexibility as well as the physical kind. The poses and postures that are used in this type of yoga practise are intended to loosen your muscles, joints and connective tissues. It can also stimulate the openness of your mind and thinking, unleashing your creative potential and allowing your mind to be a more active tool in healing you.

Kundalini yoga: For anyone who is an enthusiast of meditation or curious about incorporating meditation into yoga practice, this is an excellent type of yoga that focuses on channelling energy through the spine. It often also incorporates various breathing techniques and relaxing chanting.

How To Incorporate Crystals Into Yoga Practice

Crystals can be held or worn when you are practising any kind of yoga. They act by channelling all the positive energy that is generated by yoga poses and ensuring that your body absorbs this energy.

At the same time, the crystals will absorb any negative energy that is purged by your body when you practice yoga. This makes using crystals an extremely effective method of replacing negative energy with a more positive mental and physical state of being.

You can also incorporate crystals into the meditative part of yoga, for example when practising Kundalini yoga. You can gain significant benefits from this including:

- Lowered stress levels

- Higher cognitive functioning

- Better concentration levels

- Boosted immune system

- Elimination of negative thoughts

- Lowered blood pressure

- Relief of depression and low mood

- Increased balance in the body

- Lowered risk of insomnia

- Stabilised brainwaves

- Unblocking of creative energies

You are now ready to try a practice activity. The activity used Kundalini meditation but it can be used with other forms of yoga too. The aim is to establish an improved rhythm in your body that can promote natural healing, become more self-aware and declutter your spirit.

Practice

1. This practice activity can take place anywhere and anytime but it is important to try your best to locate a calm and quiet place where there are no distractions. Locate somewhere that is temperate so you will not be distracted by enduring the "wrong" temperature.

You can perform this meditation outside, if you want, such as in a place that makes you feel close to the earth or the water. If you are a spiritual person and you find that you draw a lot of positive energy from these natural sources, then it is preferable to be as close to the earth or water as possible.

2. Selecting the correct attire is also extremely important because you need to feel comfortable. The colour of your clothes can also be instrumental in promoting the healing results that you seek.

   Generally, you should aim to opt for light colours such as white, yellow or orange. These colours promote a sense of lightness, brightness and positivity. Stay away from darker colours and black clothes as these are more heavily associated with dark and negative energy, which is the opposite of the objective you are trying to achieve.

3. Identifying your objective is an important step before you get started on the meditation. To be able to heal yourself through the crystals and

meditative practice, scan your mind and body to determine where the problem lies.

For example, if you have noticed that you are experiencing regular stress headaches, then this would be the negative energy that you want to purge. You can cleanse yourself of the negativity that is leading to stress and ultimately causing your headaches.

4. Select your crystals. Choose a crystal that is appropriate to rectify your problem and can help you to achieve your objective. You can experiment with different crystals to find the one that is most in tune with your energy field.

As an example, if you have been finding yourself emotionally lost and ungrounded, try using black or green onyx to centre yourself and achieve a higher level of emotional stability.

5. Picking the best time to practice is down to personal choice and preference, but it's always best to find an opportunity when you can be alone

and you will not be disrupted or disturbed by outside influences.

You can perform this cleansing meditative yoga practice more than once a day if need be. You can also tackle different problems during different meditation sessions. You may want to boost your energy in the mornings and relax before bed.

6. Once you have everything in position and you have completed your preparation, it is time to get started on the activity itself. You may want to use meditation music in the background when you perform this activity, but that is optional. It's wise to experiment with and without music to see what works more effectively for you.

Take your crystal in your hands or wear jewellery that contains your chosen crystal. If your stone is large or you are using several smaller stones you can simply set them in front of you or lay them onto your lap.

You can either sit down on the floor and cross your legs or sit in a chair with your legs bend and resting on the ground in front of you. If you choose to sit on the floor, aim to sit on a carpet, rug, blanket or large pillow to keep you comfortable.

Ensure that your spine is entirely straight and not bent over or curves. Even more importantly, do not lie down. Whichever position you choose, make sure that you feel comfortable and restful in it.

Shut your eyes but do not screw them closed as this would make your facial muscles tense, which is not what you want. Scan your body again, ensuring that all your muscles are relaxed and you are not holding tension in areas like your forehead, arms or spine.

7. One of the best things about this activity is that you can practise it for as short or long a time as you want. It's a good idea to start with shorter practices and build up to longer and more enduring practices.

Many experienced yogis will practice their meditations for two or three hours at a time. However, you can start with a three-minute practice and build up to ten or fifteen minutes.

8. It is a good idea to chant along with the practice, using a mantra. You can use your own mantra or choose one that is often used by yogis such as "sat nam." In Sanskrit, this means "I see truth as my identity."

    You can use other affirmations, such as "I'm happy", "I'm healthy", "I'm free", "I'm smart" or any other that you choose. In general, you should stick to a two-word mantra and try to keep the words short. This is because you will repeat one word on inhalation of your breath and the other word when you exhale.

    Mantras are an excellent way to keep you mindful and help you retain your focus during your practice. If you notice that your mind starts to drift off or that intrusive thoughts creep into your mind, your mantra is a great way to refocus yourself and bring you back to the moment.

9. Move your focus to your breathing. Concentrate and the rise and fall of your chest. Think about the rhythm of your breath and its regularity.

    Every time you breathe in, recite the first word of your mantra in your head. Every time you breathe out, recite the second word of your mantra in your head. Visualise the bright light of your crystal and concentrate on breathing in this positive energy that is filling the space around you. With every exhalation, visualise any negative energy or toxicity leaving your body and mind.

    As you continue the exercise, you will notice that your breathing starts to slow and your chest will relax. Continue the cycle, keeping yourself focused on your breath and your mantra.

10. When you have established a gradual, consistent breathing rhythm, it is the right time to allow your breath and the crystal's healing energy to flow throughout your body.

    Think of your breath flowing up to your head, cleansing your mind. It flows down your arms, through your shoulders, elbows, wrists, hands and fingers, detoxing your body of negativity, anxiety, stress and pain. Focus on how the positive energy and your breath both flow down through your stomach to your lower body, with the negative energy behind purged through your feet and toes.

11. When you come to the end of your predetermined time for meditating, place the palms of your hands together, inhale and exhale deeply. Give yourself a few moments to fully come back to wakeful consciousness before you stand up.

Spend some time focusing on the feelings in your body and mind post-meditation by using a body scan. You will notice that your body and spirit both feel lighter and more relaxed. Your energy should now be more positive and it should flow more freely.

An important point to note is that this activity is not intended to provide immediate relief. You will need to establish a consistent routine of practising this activity and you will reap gradual benefits from it. This is a mind cleansing activity to purge the negativity and give your positive thoughts room to flourish.

If you can, try this activity every morning so that you begin your day with a fresh mind. You can also practise this pose, meditation and use of your crystals in the evening before bed to help calm your thoughts and create a restful environment that promotes restful sleep. Ultimately, it will balance you and ensure that your chakras are clear, your energies are in balance and your mind is optimised for your daily activities or nightly sleep.

Conclusion

Crystals can be used in a variety of ways to heal yourself, cleanse your blocked energy and ward off negative forces around you. As you have learned during the course of this book, they can be used on their own or in combination with other effective, alternative techniques to free your mind and body, opening yourself to a healthier body and a world of possibilities.

Learning to efficiently use your crystals can take time and practice. Expertise is acquired and does not occur overnight, so it is essential to persevere even if you do not see results immediately. Healing is a gradual process that entails removing negative energy and retuning your body and mind to accept the healing abilities of your crystals.

Crystal healing is a journey. As a beginner, you are embarking on a wonderful, beautiful path that will help you to unleash the hidden power of crystals and unlock their ability to heal your body and your mind.

When you are practising crystal healing, one of the best things you can do is to experiment with a variety of techniques. Every individual benefits differently from the various types of techniques and their array of crystals. What works well for one person might not work for someone else and vice versa, so you need to follow your own path, learning and adapting to what works well for you.

Most importantly of all, you should enjoy your foray into the world of crystals and their healing properties. Embrace your stones, respect them and bond with them. They can help you to find harmony, heal and enjoy a happier, more creative and more successful life in all areas.

Disclaimer

This book contains opinions and ideas of the author and is meant to teach the reader informative and helpful knowledge while due care should be taken by the user in the application of the information provided. The instructions and strategies are possibly not right for every reader and there is no guarantee that they work for everyone. Using this book and implementing the information/recipes therein contained is explicitly your own responsibility and risk. This work with all its contents does not guarantee correctness, completion, quality, or correctness of the provided information. Misinformation or misprints cannot be completely eliminated.

Printed in Great Britain
by Amazon

65727900R00066